YOUR BODY BATTLES A
SKINNED KNEE

WRITTEN BY **VICKI COBB** PHOTOMICROGRAPHS BY **DENNIS KUNKEL**

ILLUSTRATIONS BY **ANDREW N. HARRIS**

M Millbrook Press / Minneapolis

NOTE: The photomicrographs in this book were taken with a scanning electron microscope (SEM). The photos are originally in black and white. A computer program is used to add color, often to highlight interesting features. The colors used do not show the real colors of the subject. The × followed by a number indicates magnification. For example, ×250 means the object in the picture is 250 times larger than its real size.

The author gratefully acknowledges the help of Mary Slamin and Gail Fell, children's librarians from the Greenburgh Public Library.

For Jillian Davis Cobb —VC

This series is dedicated to my mom, Carmen Kunkel, for the care she gives her children and grandchildren —DK

To Adam and Leah, and all the members of the Flag Club —ANH

Millbrook Press
A division of Lerner Publishing Group, Inc.
241 First Avenue North
Minneapolis, MN 55401 U.S.A.

Website address: www.lernerbooks.com

Library of Congress Cataloging-in-Publication Data

Cobb, Vicki.
　　　Your body battles a skinned knee / by Vicki Cobb ; with photomicrographs by Dennis Kunkel ; illustrations by Andrew N. Harris.
　　　　　p. cm. — (Body Battles)
　　　Includes bibliographical references and index.
　　　ISBN 978-0-8225-6814-8 (lib. bdg. : alk. paper)
　　　1. Knee—Wounds and injuries—Juvenile literature. 2. Skin—Microbiology—Juvenile literature. 3. Wound healing—Juvenile literature. I. Harris, Andrew, 1977– ill. II. Title.
　　　RD561.C64 2009
　　　617.5'82044—dc22   2008002826

Manufactured in the United States of America
1 2 3 4 5 6 – DP – 14 13 12 11 10 09

Don't you just hate to skin your knee? First comes the pain, then the howl, and maybe even tears. But don't worry. If you take care of your scrape, your amazing body will take care of you. Different parts of your body work together as a team to help you recover—and fast! Meet the superheroes of your own body. This book tells their story.

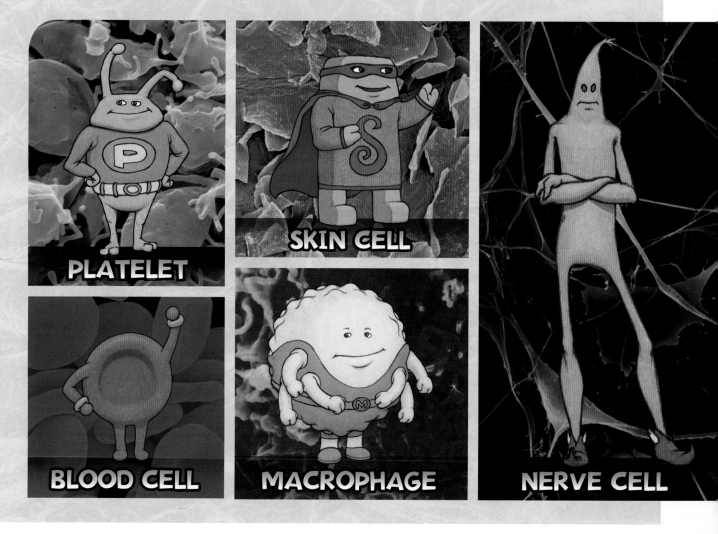

PLATELET

SKIN CELL

BLOOD CELL

MACROPHAGE

NERVE CELL

Your whole body is made of tiny living things called cells. Cells are so small that they can only be seen with a microscope—a very powerful magnifying glass.

The skin cells in this photomicrograph, made with an electron microscope, are dead and will be shed. Most of the dust in a house comes from dead human skin cells.

HUMAN SKIN

✕750

NERVE CELL   MUSCLE CELLS

BONE CELLS   RED BLOOD CELLS

Your body has many
kinds of cells that do different jobs.
Skin cells form the outer and inner surfaces of your
body. Nerve cells carry messages to and from your
brain. Muscle cells let you move and bone cells help
build your bones. Red blood cells bring oxygen
to all the cells so they can each do their job.

Skinning your knee tears through skin cells. Next nerves send
a pain message to your brain. This pain is important because
it gets your attention. It's one way your body tells you,
"Take care of me, right now!"

OUCH!

Nerves connect all parts of your body to your brain. They are like one-way telephone wires. When you skin your knee, these nerves operate at high speed—more than 200 miles (322 km) an hour. You feel the pain almost instantly.

×4,890 NERVE CELLS

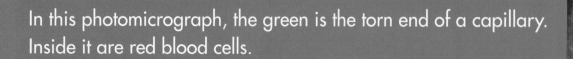

×10,000

In this photomicrograph, the green is the torn end of a capillary.
Inside it are red blood cells.

Skinning your knee also rips open the cells that make up the tiny tubes, or blood vessels, that hold your blood. Since your blood is a liquid, it spills out and you bleed.

Red blood cells are very small. A red blood cell looks like a doughnut with a dent instead of a hole. Every drop of blood contains about five million red cells floating in a clear liquid. Your blood is red because most of your blood cells are red.

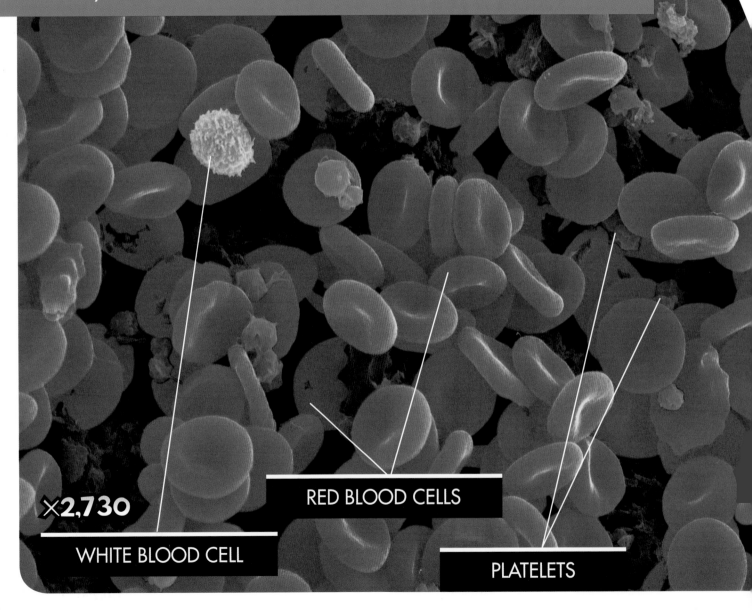

×2,730

WHITE BLOOD CELL

RED BLOOD CELLS

PLATELETS

Your body will not let you lose a lot of blood from a skinned knee. The injured skin cells give off a kind of juice that acts like an alarm bell to set off an amazing chain of events. You will soon stop bleeding and start to heal. The blood itself starts the process.

In addition to red cells, every drop of blood also contains about 200,000 platelets. Platelets are tiny pieces of cells. They are even smaller than red blood cells. They are like an army that works to slow down the bleeding.

When you start to bleed, your platelets begin sticking to the walls of your injured blood vessels and skin. They also stick to one another. As they pile up, they form a temporary plug to slow down the bleeding.

Platelets don't look like little plates. They have a jagged shape with lots of threadlike ends sticking out. That's why they are so sticky.

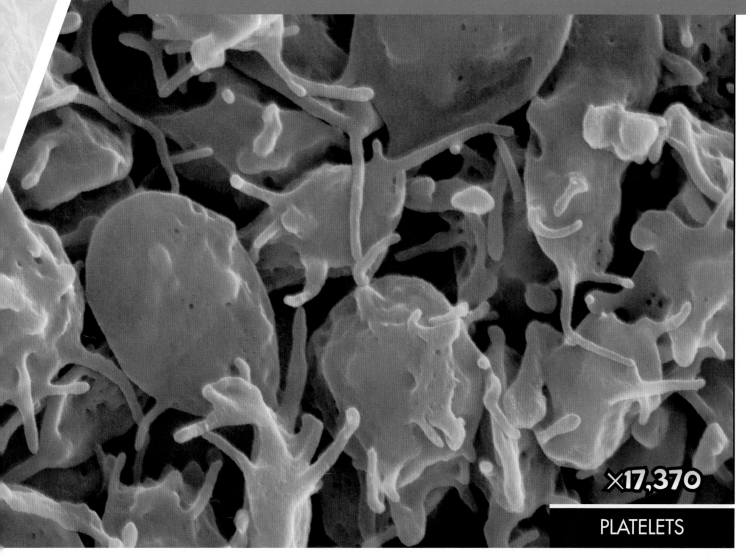

×17,370

PLATELETS

Chemicals given off by the platelets and the injured skin cells cause the formation of tiny little threads called fibrin. Fibrin threads form a tangle that traps the red cells. This is called a blood clot. In a small cut, your blood clots within two minutes.

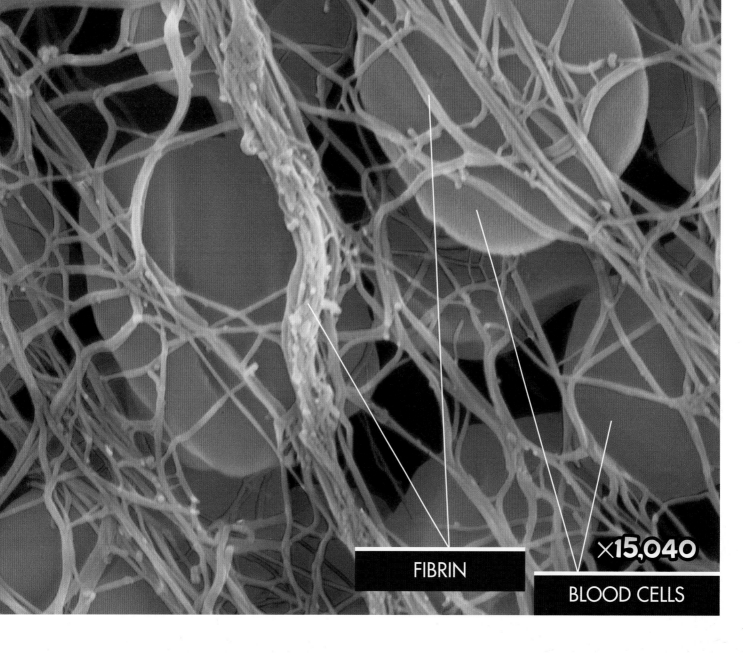

Blood must remain a liquid while it's flowing through your blood vessels. Fibrin appears only when it must form a clot to stop the bleeding.

×15,040

FIBRIN

BLOOD CELLS

When air hits a blood clot, it gradually gets tough and hard. Then it is called a scab. The scab protects you. It stays on your knee while the skin repairs itself. New cells replace the ones destroyed when you got hurt. When the skin is all better, the scab falls off.

✕11,900

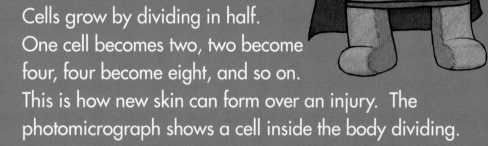

Cells grow by dividing in half.
One cell becomes two, two become
four, four become eight, and so on.
This is how new skin can form over an injury. The
photomicrograph shows a cell inside the body dividing.

Your skin not only keeps your insides inside you, it also keeps the outside from getting in. Germs, also known as bacteria, are one-celled living things. They are as small as or smaller than most of your cells. Germs can live on your skin, but they can't get through the many layers of healthy skin.

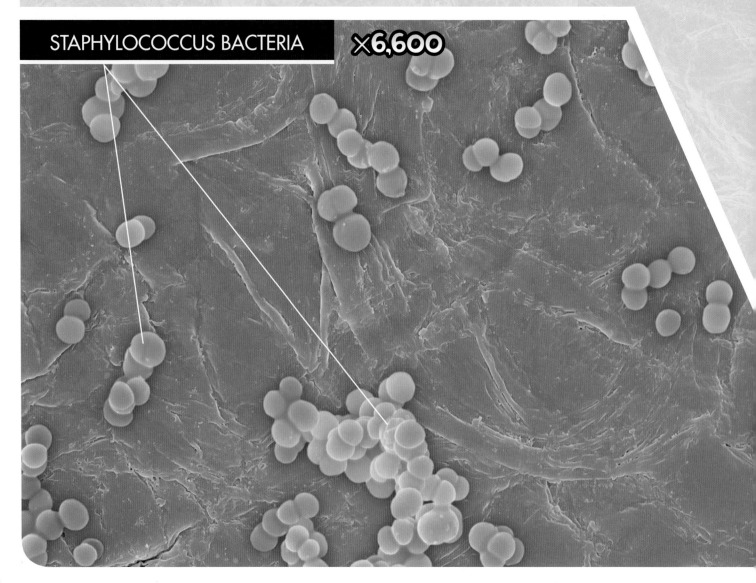

STAPHYLOCOCCUS BACTERIA ×6,600

The photomicrograph shows germs on skin. They are waiting to get inside through a mouth or nose—or through a break in the skin.

When you skin your knee, these unwanted germs have a way to get into your body. Your warm, moist insides are the perfect place to help them grow and multiply!

An invasion of germs into your body causes an infection. The germs destroy your cells when they grow and multiply. But you have ways to fight back. A battle takes place inside your body.

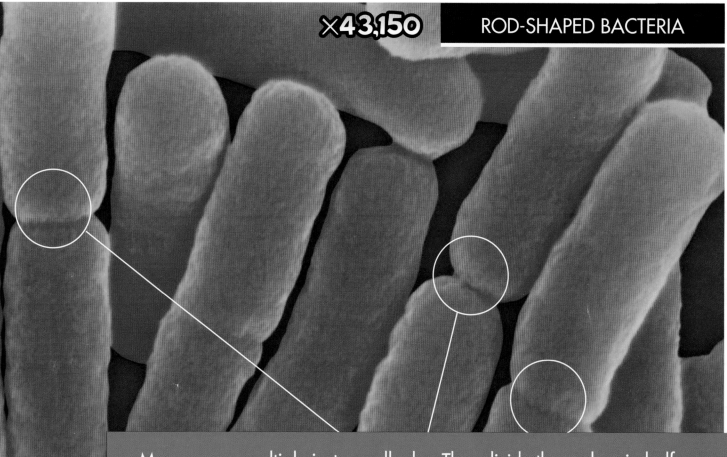

×43,150   **ROD-SHAPED BACTERIA**

Many germs multiply just as cells do. They divide themselves in half as shown here. Some germs divide every 20 minutes. It takes a day or two before there are enough germs to cause an infection.

Of course, your body doesn't take a germ invasion lying down! Blood rushes in to help. This makes the area around the wound swell up and get red. Swelling acts as a wall around the infection. It keeps the germs from moving farther into your body.

The pressure from the swelling is painful, and your wound feels sore. This soreness is a signal from your body that your injury needs attention. Then big, bumpy germ-eating cells called macrophages swing into action.

Macrophages are a kind of white blood cell. They clean up infections by grabbing and devouring bacteria.

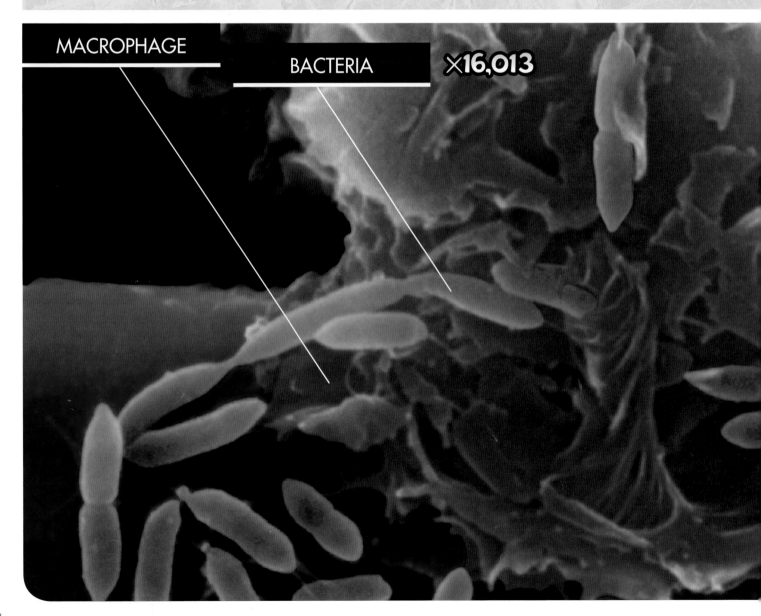

MACROPHAGE

BACTERIA

×16,013

When a macrophage meets up with a germ,
the macrophage's ridged knobs surround it.
The macrophage draws the germ inside where
its powerful juices digest it.

Macrophages have to work fast gobbling up germs. Multiplying germs give off irritating and sometimes harmful juices. Macrophages can eat just so many germs before they themselves die. Dead macrophages show up as pus in infections.

Macrophages are like garbage trucks cleaning up the debris left after an infection. Not only do they get rid of the dead germs, but they will eat the dead macrophages. While all this is going on, your injury is swollen and still feels sore.

So when you skin your knee, you don't want to give the germs a chance to get inside you. That's why you wash your wound, disinfect it with hydrogen peroxide or iodine to kill the germs, put ointment on it, and cover it with a bandage to keep it clean.

If the germs don't get in, your body forms a clean scab and you won't get an infection. In a few days, you'll win the battle against the germs—without ever having to think much about it.

GLOSSARY

bacteria: one-celled microorganisms that live with other living things. Some bacteria are helpful, but others cause disease.

blood clot: liquid blood that has turned into a solid mass

blood vessels: Tubes that carry blood. Veins carry blood back to the heart, arteries carry blood from the heart to the rest of the body. Capillaries connect arteries and veins.

cell: the smallest unit of a living thing that is alive

disinfectant: a substance that can kill germs

fibrin: fibers formed by blood when it clots

germs: one-celled organisms that cause disease, including bacteria and viruses

hydrogen peroxide: a disinfectant that kills germs by flooding them with oxygen

iodine: a disinfectant that kills germs by poisoning them

macrophage: a white blood cell that cleans up sick and infected areas by "eating" germs and dead cells

microscope: a powerful magnifier that allows us to look at cells. There are two main kinds of microscopes:

electron microscopes use electrons and can magnify even smaller structures. There are two types of electron microscopes—scanning (SEM), which can magnify up to 500,000 times, and transmission (TEM), which can magnify up to one million times.

optical microscopes use light and can magnify up to 1,500 times the actual size.

muscle cells: the smallest structures of muscle tissue capable of contracting

nerve cells: One of a group of cells, also known as neurons, whose function is to process and send information throughout the body.

photomicrograph: a photograph taken through a microscope

platelets: partial cells found in the blood that start the process of clotting. Some scientists refer to them as cells without a nucleus.

red blood cells: the cells in the blood responsible for carrying oxygen to all parts of the body.

scab: a dried blood clot that has been exposed to the air

skin cells: cells that make up the outer and inner surfaces of the body

white blood cells: colorless cells floating in the blood that help fight disease

FURTHER READING

Balestrino, Philip. *The Skeleton Inside You.* Rev. ed. New York: HarperCollins, 1989.

Mitchell, Melanie. *Killing Germs.* Minneapolis: Lerner Publications Company, 2006.

Rau, Dana Meachen. *What's Inside Me?: My Heart and Blood.* New York: Benchmark Books, 2004.

Royston, Angela. *Why Do Bruises Change Color? And Other Questions about Blood.* Chicago: Heinemann Library, 2002.

Showers, Paul. *A Drop of Blood.* Rev. ed. New York: HarperCollins, 2004.

Silverstein, Alvin, and Virginia Silverstein, and Laura Silverstein Nunn. *Cuts, Scrapes, Scabs, and Scars.* Danbury, CT: Franklin Watts, 2000.

Storad, Conrad J. *The Circulatory System.* Minneapolis: Lerner Publications Company, 2005.

WEBSITES

The Epic Story of Blood from Public Broadcasting:
http://www.pbs.org/wnet/redgold/index.html
An animated chart of blood traveling through the circulatory system is featured.

The Franklin Institute
http://sln.fi.edu/biosci/blood/blood.html
This site offers a number of fascinating facts about blood.

How Stuff Works
http://health.howstuffworks.com/define-platelets.htm
How platelets help blood to coagulate is explained.

Washington State University
http://www.wsu.edu/DrUniverse/wounds.html
How wounds heal is clearly explained.

INDEX